Getting a Life of Your Own:

A Kid's Guide to Understanding and Coping with Family Alcoholism

by

Kim "Tip" Frank, Ed.S., LPC
Counselor/Psychotherapist
Rock Hill School District
Family Counseling and
   Play Therapy Services
Rock Hill, SC

Susan J. Smith-Rex, Ed.D.
School of Education
Winthrop University
Rock Hill, SC

Illustrations coordinated by Stephan E. Frank
Cover drawing by John Varkis

Copyright 1995
Educational Media Corporation®
P.O. Box 21311
Minneapolis, MN 55421-0311

(612) 781-0088

ISBN 0-932796-73-7

Library of Congress Catalog No. 95-60564

Printing (Last Digit)

9 8 7 6 5 4 3 2 1

Educational Media Corporation® reserves all rights to the materials in this book under U.S. copyright laws. In an effort to provide educational materials which are as practical and economical as possible, we grant to *individual* purchasers of this book the right to make copies of material contained therein for their personal use only. This permission is *limited* to a single person, and does not apply to entire schools or school systems. Additional copies of this book should be purchased for each teacher or counselor for use with their students. Copying this book or its parts for resale is strictly prohibited.

Production editor—

Don L. Sorenson, Ph.D.

Graphic Design—

Earl Sorenson

Illustrations—

The following students at Mariner High School in Cape Coral, Florida, under the direction of Stephan E. Frank, are the illustrators: Jason Blakeney, Jeremy Domby, Katherine Gillen, Lena Abdel Jaber, Selena Poppell, Scott Rigby, John Varkis, and Jessica Wilson.

Special Thanks—

To Dr. Jan Shaw, Dr. Mitsuko Shannon, and Dr. Patricia Tonkowicz for the direction and support they provided us in the writing of this book.

Note to parents and health professionals:

This book is intended to aid children in dealing with family members' alcoholism. The book was carefully written to be user friendly for children. We trust the vocabulary, illustrations, and limited number of words on each page will make this book inviting and helpful to children in their understanding of alcoholism.

The second part of this book focuses on practical ideas children can use to better cope with family alcoholism. We believe in children's abilities to work out problems in their own lives. This section is interactive in nature. The student selects areas of concern and does activities which will help the child to explore what needs to be done to best cope. In essence, self-care projects are provided that are practical and thought provoking.

While the book can be used independently by elementary and middle school students, we highly recommend parents and mental health professionals read and discuss this book with children. In this way the information and suggestions are fully discussed and the children are encouraged to follow through on the coping strategies provided. Best wishes as you put this book to good use!

Kim "Tip" Frank, Ed.S., LPC

Susan J. Smith-Rex, Ed. D.

Table of Contents

Forward   Note to Parents and Health Professionals 3

Part I   Helping Children Understand and Cope with Alcoholism 5

Part II   Practical Ideas to Cope with Family Alcoholism 33

        Terms 35

        1. Learning the Facts about Alcoholism 36

        2. Identifying a Support Team 41

        3. Learning Self-Protection Skills 44

        4. Feeling Better About Myself 53

        5. Taking Control of My Life 59

        References 62

Part I

Helping Children Understand and Cope with Alcoholism

Katherine Gillen

Very few people can say they don't worry about something each day.

Getting a Life of Your Own

Jason Blakeney

It is common to compare who we are or what we have with other people we know. We often spend time wishing we have what someone else has or wishing we could be someone else.

Jessica Wilson

You may believe if you wish hard enough you can become another person or make your worries disappear. The truth is you are who you are and sometimes your worries are out of your control.

What are some of the things others say they often worry about?

Someone in my family is sick.

My parent has lost his or her job.

There isn't enough money to pay the bills.

One of my parents is always in a bad mood.

My parents are getting a divorce.

School is too hard.

I don't feel like I have enough friends.

I don't like the way I look.

I don't get along with my parents, family, or classmates.

Someone in my family takes drugs.

My parent drinks too much.

A Kid's Guide to Understanding and Coping with Family Alcoholism

Jason Blakeney

One family worry that many children today are facing is alcoholism. Many parents have an alcoholic drink occasionally, but when it happens too often and interferes with family and work responsibilities, then we call this alcoholism.

Getting a Life of Your Own

Jason Blakeney

You might see a family member's behavior change when he or she drinks too much beer, wine, or liquor. Some people get silly and loud. Others may get mean, or sleep too much. Oftentimes the person appears not to care about the feelings of others and may act in ways that embarrass you.

A Kid's Guide to Understanding and Coping with Family Alcoholism

Jason Blakeney

Roughly one out of every eight Americans is a child of an alcoholic and experiences problems due to alcohol. Children usually feel frustrated because they don't know how to make the family member stop drinking.

Getting a Life of Your Own

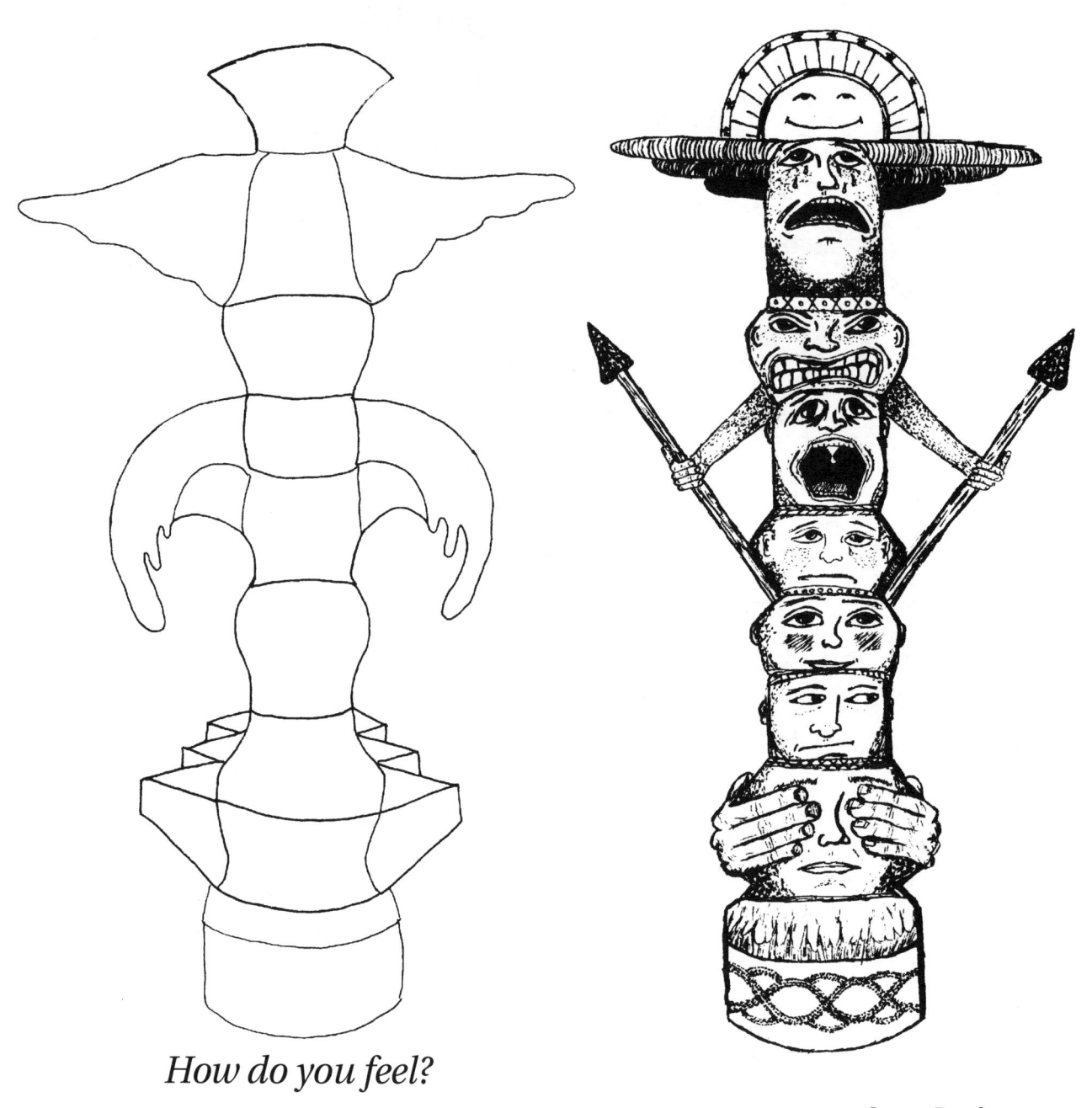

How do you feel?

Jeremy Domby

Children who see too much drinking in their home are confused about how they feel. Children may feel anger, fear, sadness, guilt, loneliness, embarrassment, unloved, or ashamed. Usually many of these emotions are felt at the same time.

A Kid's Guide to Understanding and Coping with Family Alcoholism

John Varkis

Children tend to react to their emotions by using defenses to hide their true feelings. Some of the common defenses are: joking all the time, daydreaming, talking back, hiding, blaming, constant talking, or trying to be perfect.

Jessica Wilson

When a parent or family member is sick with alcohol addiction, it affects the whole family. It doesn't matter where you live, what race you are, how much money your family has, how old you are, or whether you are a boy or girl. It can happen to anyone whose parent turns to alcohol when dealing with life's problems.

Children react to a family drinking problem in different ways.

Physical Responses	*Emotional Responses*	*Behavioral Responses*
Tense muscles	Disgusted	Daydreaming
Sweating	Angry	Acting Out
Heart Speeds Up	Depressed	Fighting
Difficulty Sleeping	Sad	Crying
Headaches	Lonely	Trying to be Perfect
Upset Stomach	Frustrated	Joking a lot
Bowel Problems	Unloved	Hiding
Loss of Appetite or Overeating	Ashamed	
	Jealous	
Bad mood	Fearful	
Ulcers	Guilty	
Tiredness	Embarrassed	

Getting a Life of Your Own

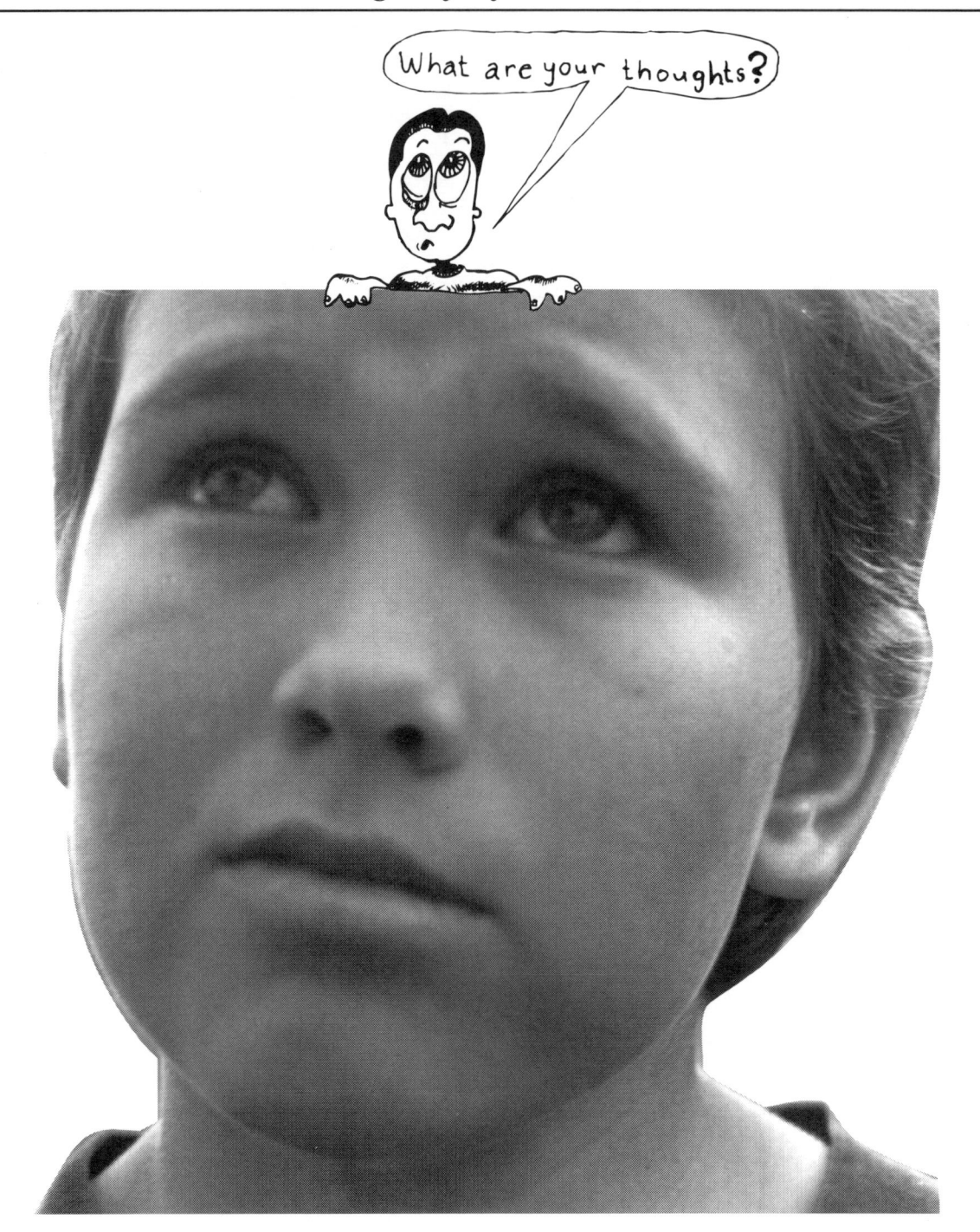

What are your thoughts?

Katherine Gillen

Oftentimes when a family is having difficulty, family members ignore the real source of the problem which is alcoholism. Family members seem to act as if there is no problem, even though it may be obvious.

18　　　　　　　　　Kim "Tip" Frank, Ed.S., LPC and Susan J. Smith-Rex, Ed.D.

A Kid's Guide to Understanding and Coping with Family Alcoholism

Scott Rigby

Three common unspoken rules are found in families where alcohol or other drugs are being used. They are:
   Don't talk
   Don't trust
   Don't feel

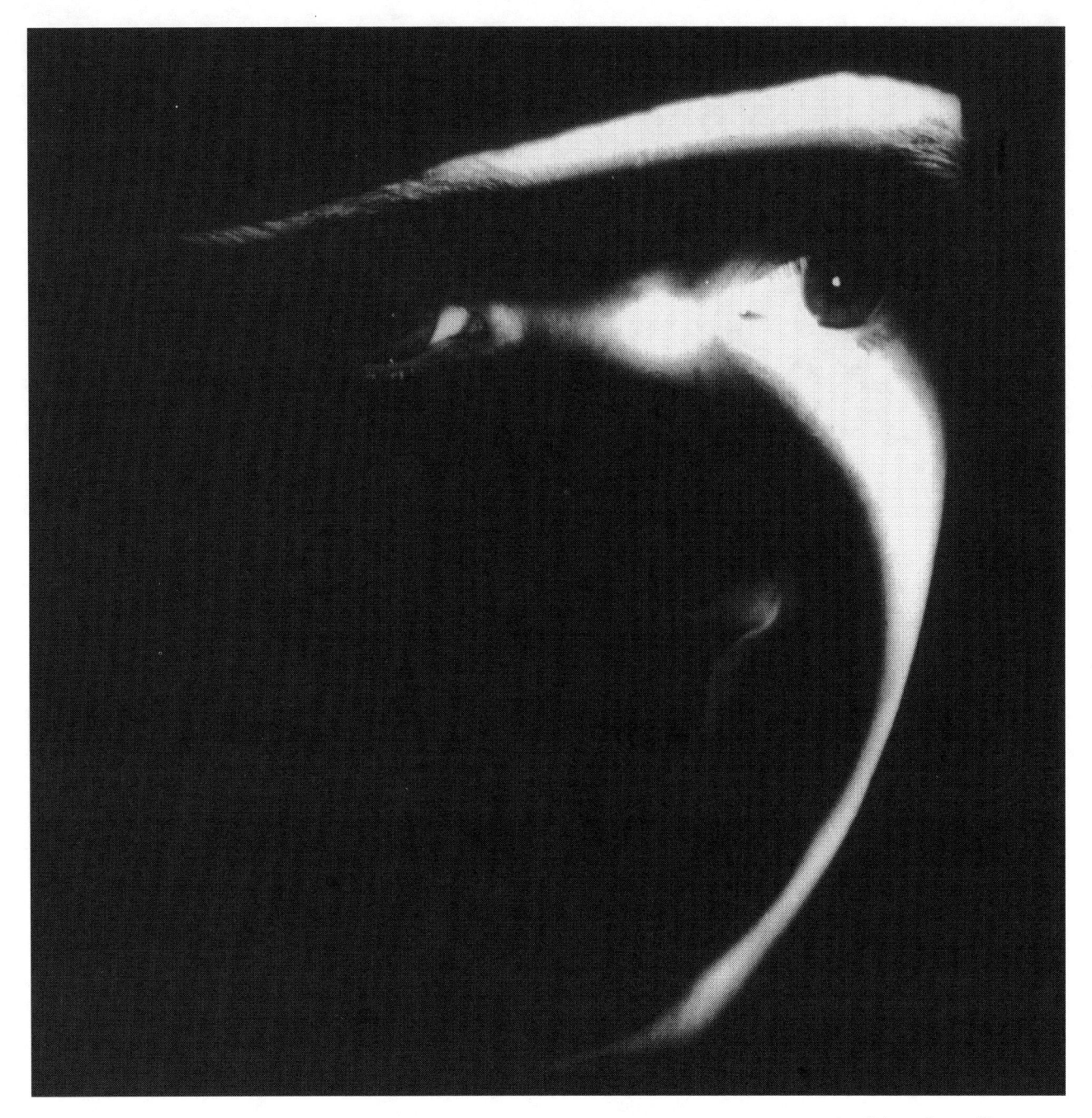

Selena Poppell

The family not only avoids or stays away from discussing the problem of alcoholism among themselves, but all others outside the family are shielded from the truth. Alcoholism becomes a family secret.

Jessica Wilson

It is not uncommon for survival roles to be used within a family. These roles are played out to avoid facing the real problem of a family member's alcoholism and to draw attention away from the family's problem.

Jason Blakeney

Survival roles may include the following:
- *The hero*
- *The rescuer or enabler*
- *The rebel or scapegoat*
- *The lost child*
- *The mascot*

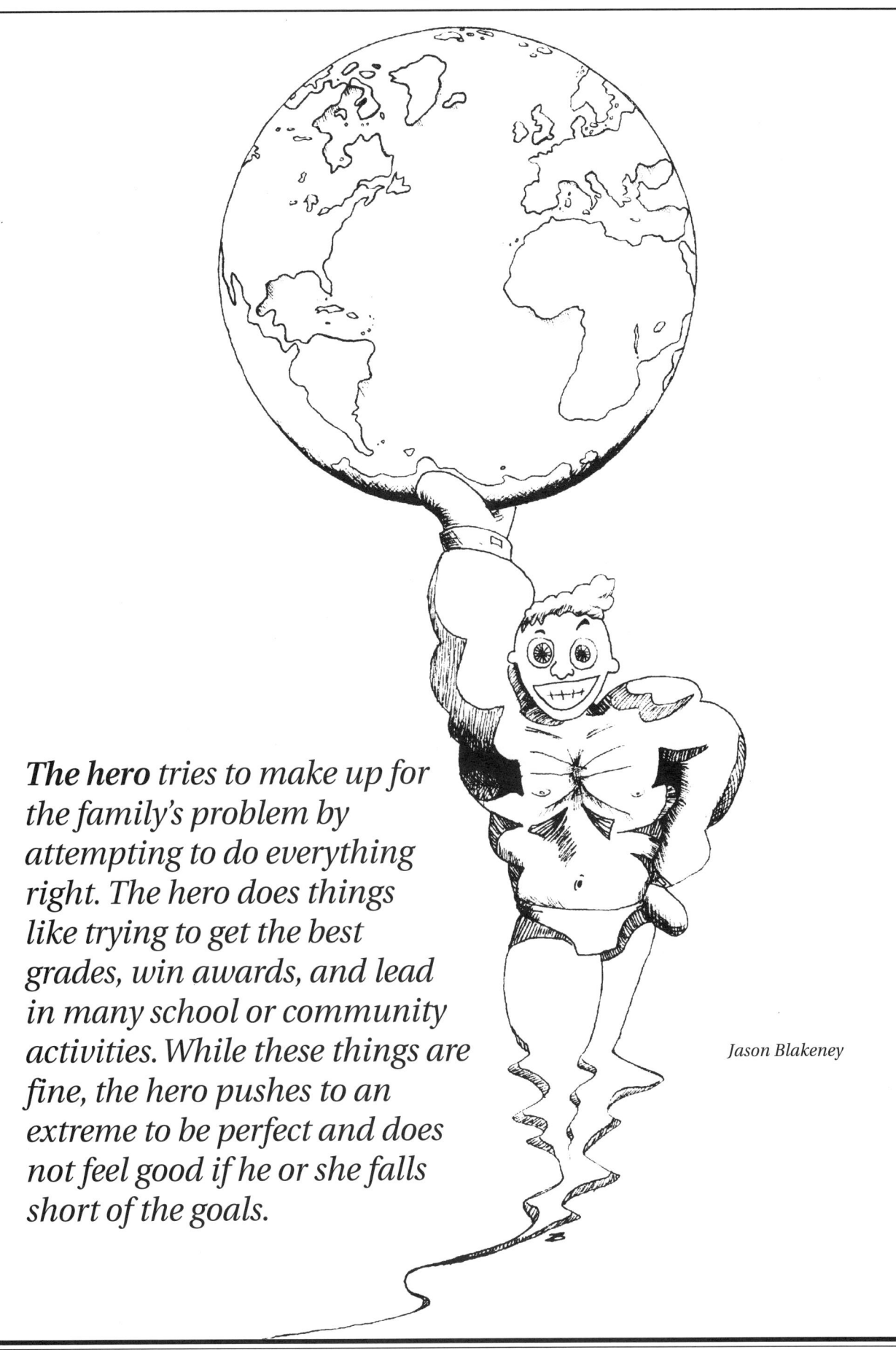

The hero *tries to make up for the family's problem by attempting to do everything right. The hero does things like trying to get the best grades, win awards, and lead in many school or community activities. While these things are fine, the hero pushes to an extreme to be perfect and does not feel good if he or she falls short of the goals.*

Jason Blakeney

Katherine Gillen

The rescuer *tries to help the alcoholic. He or she may try to hide or get rid of the alcoholic's beer, wine, or liquor. The rescuer may do jobs to cover up for the alcoholic such as cooking, cleaning the house, and making excuses for the alcoholic. Sadly enough the rescuer cannot stop the alcoholic from drinking. By taking on the responsibilities of the alcoholic, the rescuer enables the alcoholic to continue drinking without facing the consequences of the behavior, thus actually making things worse.*

Katherine Gillen

The rebel *draws attention away from the family's problems by getting into constant trouble. The rebel typically gets in fights, breaks rules, and gets poor grades. This person is often angry and seems to sacrifice himself or herself to save the family from facing the problem of alcoholism.*

Lena Abdel Jaber

The lost child *in an attempt to protect himself or herself tends to go unnoticed. He or she tends to be shy and does activities such as reading or watching TV alone. The lost child avoids the family's problems of alcoholism by quietly and safely dropping out of sight and causing few problems.*

A Kid's Guide to Understanding and Coping with Family Alcoholism

John Varkis

The mascot *tends to soften the hurt of family problems by humor. The mascot is often the class clown and makes a joke out of life in general. He or she avoids taking life seriously and survives by becoming a comedian.*

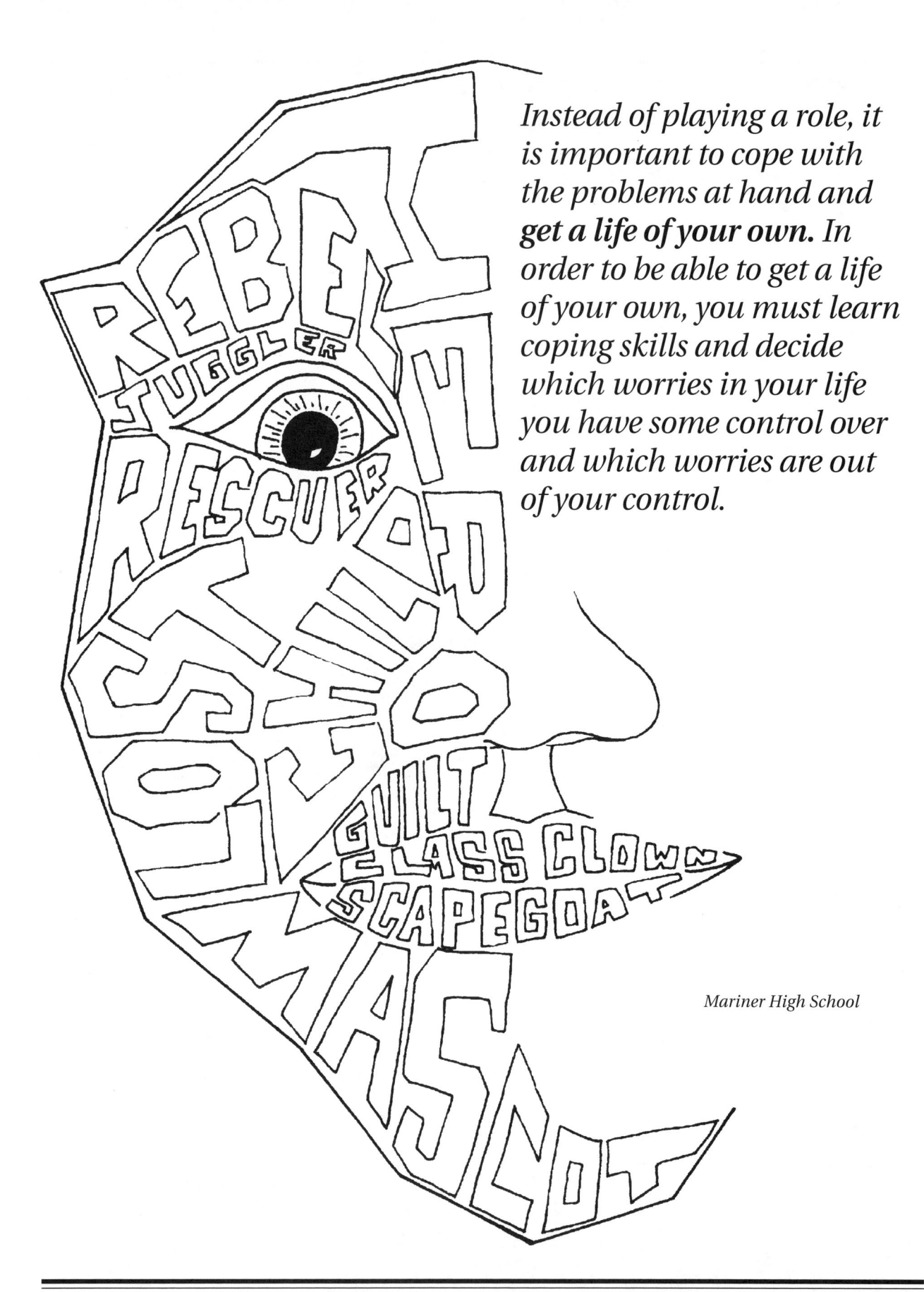

Getting a Life of Your Own

*Instead of playing a role, it is important to cope with the problems at hand and **get a life of your own**. In order to be able to get a life of your own, you must learn coping skills and decide which worries in your life you have some control over and which worries are out of your control.*

Mariner High School

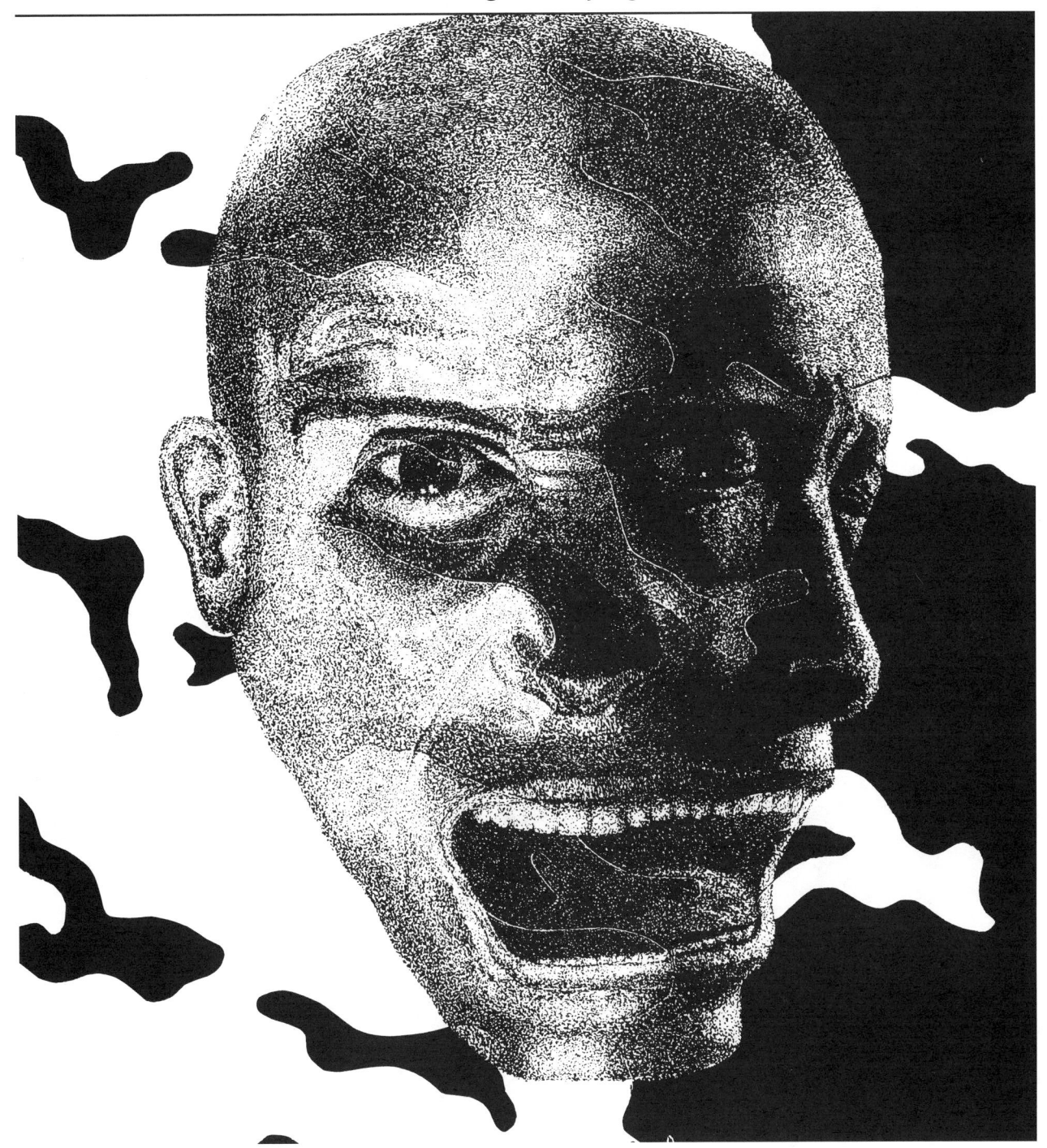

A Kid's Guide to Understanding and Coping with Family Alcoholism

Jeremy Domby

You are only responsible for your own behavior. You cannot be responsible for an adult becoming an alcoholic. You cannot cure or control your parent's sickness. You can only encourage the person to seek medical help if possible and then learn to take care of your own needs.

Educational Media Corporation®, Box 21311, Minneapolis, MN 55421-0311

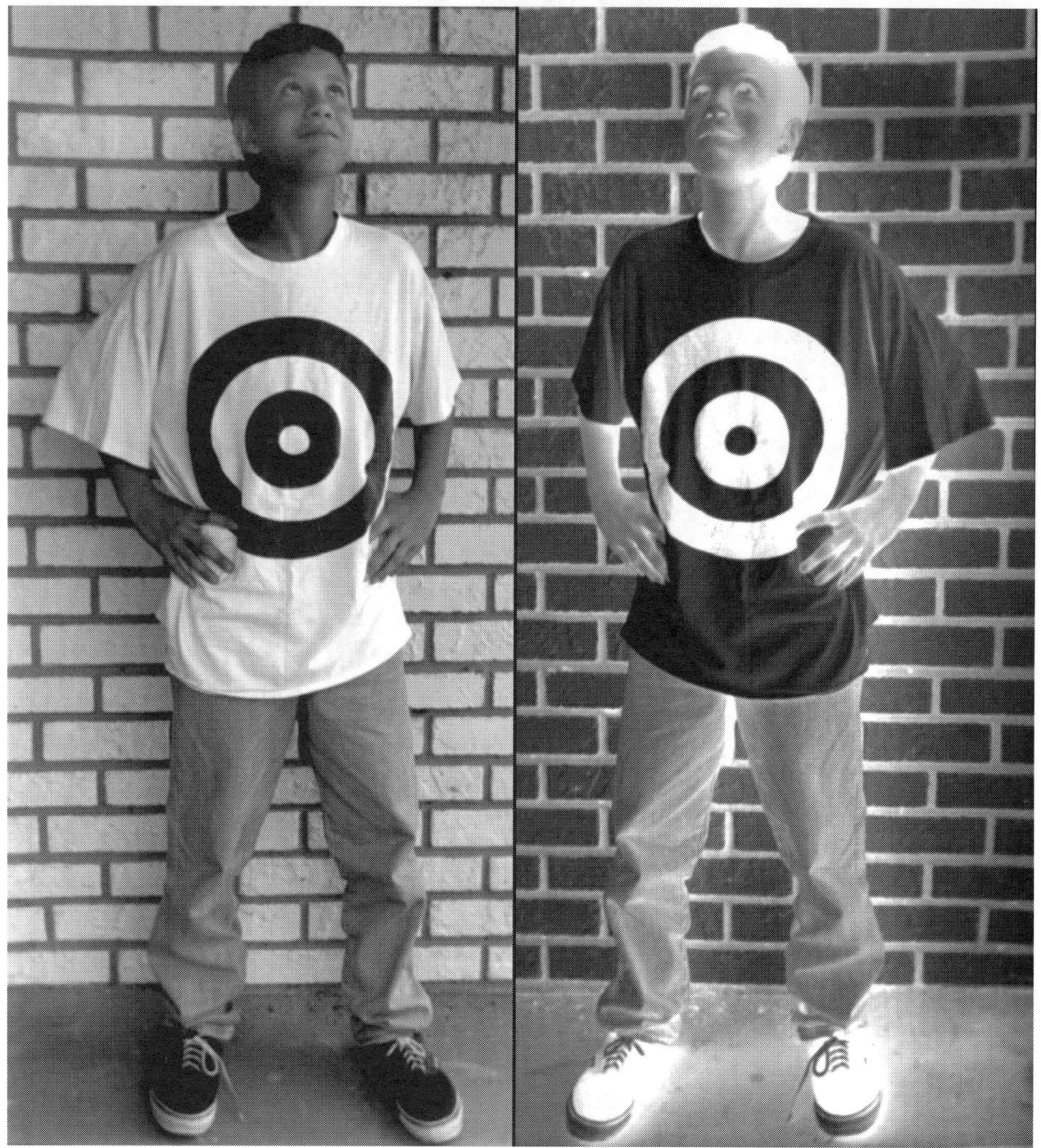

Katherine Gillen

There are four important C's to know:
1. *You didn't cause the alcoholism.*
2. *You cannot cure the problem.*
3. *You cannot control the problem, but*
4. *You can learn to cope with it.*

A Kid's Guide to Understanding and Coping with Family Alcoholism

Jeremy Domby

What does it mean to cope with a problem? This means that you learn positive ways to act so you can feel good about yourself and begin to learn how to make your life more predictable and happy.

Getting a Life of Your Own

John Varkis

Getting a life of your own means not letting someone else's problem keep you from having a life of your own. It means controlling what you can and making up your mind that things can and will get better as you go on with your own life.

Part II

Practical Ideas to Cope with Family Alcoholism

Getting a Life of Your Own

In order to better deal with a family member's alcoholism, we have identified five good things you can do to help yourself. Think about which ones you may need to consider and turn to the pages that are shown for some helpful ideas. Take good care of yourself. You're worth it.

Self-Care Projects

1. **Learning the facts about alcoholism:**
   What is alcoholism and how does it affect me?
   (Turn to page 36.)

2. **Identifying a support team:**
   Safe people I can turn to for help.
   (Turn to page 41.)

3. **Learning self-protection skills:**
   Skills and information to take care of myself.
   (Turn to page 44.)

4. **Feeling better about myself:**
   Developing a healthy self-concept and dealing with my feelings.
   (Turn to page 53.)

5. **Taking control of my life:**
   Making good choices to make my life better.
   (Turn to page 57.)

Terms

Abuse	To be treated in a wrong or hurtful way.
Addiction	When a person depends upon a drug to deal with life.
Al-Anon	An organization that helps relatives of those who have drinking problems.
Al-Ateen	An organization that helps teenagers cope with a family member's alcoholism.
Al-Atot	An organization that helps children cope with a family member's alcoholism.
Alcohol	A depressant drug that slows down the central nervous system. Alcoholic drinks are made from grains and fruits and contain the chemical ethanol. Drinks include wine, beer and hard liquor. Alcohol is the most abused drug in America.
Alcoholics Anonymous	An organization that helps people who have a drinking problem.
Alcoholism	When drinking becomes uncontrollable, the drinker is said to be suffering from alcoholism.
Anxiety	A feeling of fearful uneasiness or worry about what may happen.
At Risk	People more likely to suffer problems from living with a parent who abuses or is addicted to alcohol.
COA	Children of Alcoholics
Chemical Dependency	A strong need to drink alcohol or use other drugs to feel better about yourself or to escape from problems.
Clear Messages	When a person thinks good thoughts about himself or herself.
Coping Skills	Positive ways to act so you can feel good about yourself and begin solving your problems in living with an alcoholic parent.
Defenses	Walls we create to hide true feelings: jokes, daydreaming, talk back, silence, blaming, people pleasing, too busy, constant talking, using drugs.
Drug Abuse	The non-medical use of drugs that alter the mind.
Drug Addict	When a person is hooked on drugs.
Empathy	Attempting to understand others' feelings or ideas.
Muddy Messages	When a person thinks bad thoughts about himself or herself.
Poor Self-Esteem	When a person feels of little or no worth.
Strategy	A careful plan for achieving a goal.
Support System	Community helpers and family you know you can turn to for help.

1. Learning the Facts About Alcoholism: What is alcoholism and how does it affect me?

Mark True or False for each statement.

T F

☐ ☐ 1. Alcoholism is a disease that tends to affect everyone in the family.

☐ ☐ 2. About one in eight people who begin drinking alcohol will eventually become an alcoholic.

☐ ☐ 3. Children of alcoholics are four times more likely than other children to become alcoholics later in life.

☐ ☐ 4. Daughters of alcoholics tend to marry alcoholics when they grow up.

☐ ☐ 5. Approximately one-fifth of the children in a typical classroom are growing up in a drug or alcohol dependent family.

☐ ☐ 6. Children of alcoholics are more likely to complain of illnesses and be absent from school.

☐ ☐ 7. Children of alcoholics are more likely to abuse drugs (including alcohol), drop out of school, and suffer from depression.

☐ ☐ 8. Children of alcoholics often feel like failures because they can't stop their parents from drinking.

☐ ☐ 9. Alcoholism plays a large part in about 90% of reported child abuse cases.

☐ ☐ 10. Most children of alcoholics (95%,) pass through school without ever receiving assistance for this problem.

Source: "Children of Alcoholics: Facts and Figures," *The Big Issue*.

As you may have guessed, the answers to all of these statements are *true*. Children of alcoholics are greatly affected, which makes it *important* for you to explore what you can do to cope. One of the first steps is gaining an understanding of just how much alcoholism can affect you now and in the future. The first step is to face it and then to figure out what to do about it. Try this. We call it FADD, which is a great way to cope with any problem.

FADD

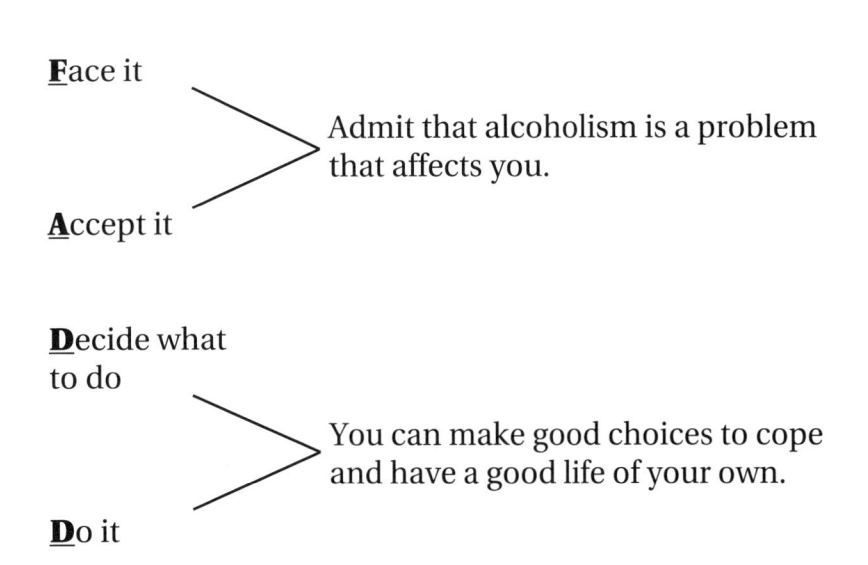

Face it

Accept it

> Admit that alcoholism is a problem that affects you.

Decide what to do

Do it

> You can make good choices to cope and have a good life of your own.

Alcohol has a powerful grip on the alcoholic. At a certain point, alcoholics are powerless or unable to stop drinking unless they seek help. Even though the alcoholic may see the alcohol is ruining his or her life, that person may still be unable to stop drinking. The addiction to alcohol controls the alcoholic. He or she has an abnormal reaction to alcohol.

To help you understand *what* overcoming an addiction is like, try the following activity. This exercise may give you a feel for what it is like to try to stop something you are used to doing.

Empathy Exercise

Procedure:

Pick one habit or activity in your life that would be very difficult to stop doing. (See the list of examples on the next page.) Sign a contract to discontinue the activity for at least one week. At the end of the week, think about what the experience was like by answering the following questions. Be honest with your answers.

1. How successful were you?

2. Did you cheat at all? Did anyone catch you? How did you feel?

3. Did you miss your habit? What feelings were you experiencing?

4. Did you substitute your forbidden habit with a substitute activity?

5. Did you treat your family and friends differently?

6. Did you start doing things that you don't usually do?

7. Did you have a friend or support team help you to break your habit? Did it help to be with someone else who was also refraining from a very enjoyable activity?

8. How do you think your feelings are like those of an addict?

9. Based on this exercise, how do you think addicted people can best be helped?

Contract

I _____ have decided to give up
     (Name)

_____

(Activity or Habit)

for a period of one week.

Examples you might select from:

1. Stop biting fingernails.

2. Give up sweets.

3. Give up a special activity (riding bikes, playing Nintendo).

4. Neither make nor answer any telephone calls.

5. Stop watching TV or listening to the radio.

6. Give up soda (soft drinks).

7. Give up a favorite sport.

8. Give up gum.

_____

Signature of Commitment

Getting a Life of Your Own

It is also important to understand *why* alcoholics act the way they do. While it is impossible to understand all the reasons behind their behavior, gaining an understanding of what is happening physically to the alcoholic may give you some insight. Try the following activity to better imagine what it may be like to have an addiction to a drug such as alcohol.

Spin Exercise

Have a friend carefully, but quickly, turn you around and around for fifteen seconds. (Stay away from any objects that may cause injury.) Then sit in a comfortable chair.

This experience may be similar to what happens when one loses control because of alcohol abuse. List feelings you had after the spin activity.

1.
2.
3.
4.
5.

The behaviors and feelings of the alcoholic are similar to the ones you experienced during and after the Spin Activity.

They may include:

1. Being confused
2. Irritability (grouchiness)
3. Anger
4. Acting silly
5. Undependable (not being able to do normal things that need to be done)
6. Out of control (does unreasonable things)

No doubt these behaviors and feelings have an effect on the whole family. Sections two and three will discuss finding support and how to protect yourself. Read on!

2. Identifying a Support Team: Safe People I Can Turn to for Help

Community Support Groups

It is not always possible to talk to family members about their problem of alcoholism. Therefore, it is nice to know there is help all around you. Hopefully, as you learn to cope with the problem at home, family members may be more open to talking directly about the problem. You and other family members can receive help from community groups such as:

Al-Anon	Al-Anon is a support group for family members living with an alcoholic.
Al-Ateen	Al-Ateen helps teenagers find encouragement and practical help in dealing with a family member's alcoholism.
Al-Atot	Al-Atot helps younger children learn to cope with a family member's alcoholism.
Alcoholics Anonymous	AA helps the alcoholic stop drinking and remain alcohol free. AA is a great resource when the alcoholic does want help.

Alcoholics can and do recover every day. In the community resource section of your local phone book, the names and numbers of community agencies are listed. Look under the heading of alcohol abuse. Don't be afraid to call for help.

Support at School

In your school, there is likely a support group for children of alcoholics. Ask your counselor or a teacher for information about small group counseling. Support groups help you to see that you are not the only one dealing with the problem of alcoholism and its effects on the family. Many kids your age meet to encourage each other and to discuss ideas for coping. The group offers a safe place for you to vent your feelings and to enjoy being with others.

Safe People

Just as important as an ongoing support group are individuals with whom you feel comfortable discussing your situation. These are called safe people because they are ones you can count on to be trusted and helpful. It is a good idea to build a network of safe people, both adults and children. Trusted adults may include a parent, coach, teacher, counselor, best friend's mother, religious leader, and so forth.

Friendships with peers may grow out of the support group and other activities in which you may participate. Clubs and after school activities are a good way to develop friendships and to take pressure off from an unpleasant situation at home.

What does your support team look like? Fill in as many circles as possible. Be sure to include individuals and groups who are helpful to you. Remember, you don't have to be the "Lone Ranger." There are many people who care. You can develop your support team as large as you would like. It seems to gradually grow as you reach out.

Individuals and Groups That Make Up My Support Team

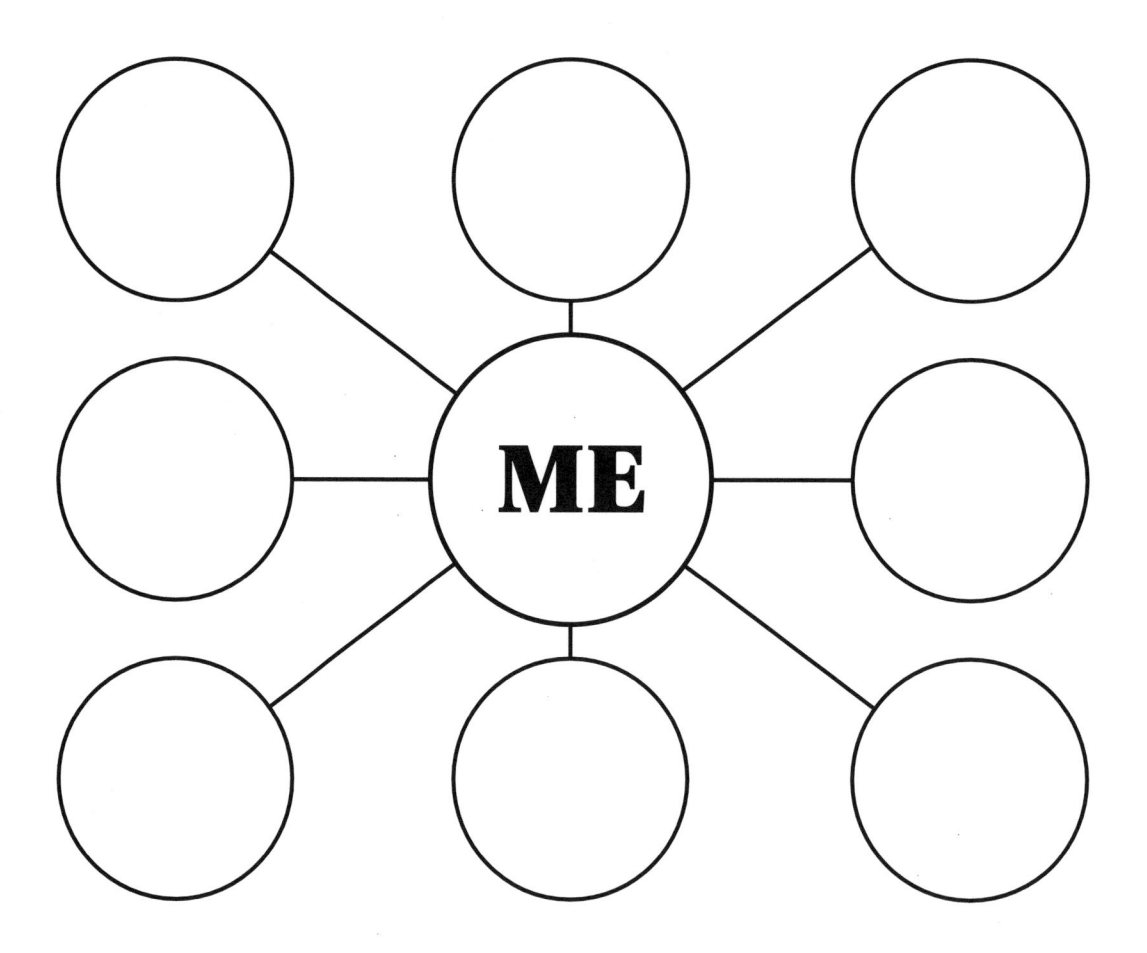

A Kid's Guide to Understanding and Coping with Family Alcoholism

Where to Turn?

Identifying Your Support System

Think about the following situations. Check the boxes of those with whom you would most likely feel comfortable discussing the matter.

parent	friend	teacher	counselor	school nurse	church	doctor	alcohol and drug centers	resources in telephone book	youth service	telephone 911 in emergencies	a relative	Other		Situation
❑	❑	❑	❑	❑	❑	❑	❑	❑	❑	❑	❑	❑	1.	A family member was drinking and has threatened to leave home.
❑	❑	❑	❑	❑	❑	❑	❑	❑	❑	❑	❑	❑	2.	You feel embarrassed about your parent's drinking, which makes it hard to develop friendships.
❑	❑	❑	❑	❑	❑	❑	❑	❑	❑	❑	❑	❑	3.	Your grades have fallen because you've been upset about your situation at home.
❑	❑	❑	❑	❑	❑	❑	❑	❑	❑	❑	❑	❑	4.	You're being spanked at home much more than you think is necessary.
❑	❑	❑	❑	❑	❑	❑	❑	❑	❑	❑	❑	❑	5.	Sometimes you're alone in the evenings and you feel lonely and scared.
❑	❑	❑	❑	❑	❑	❑	❑	❑	❑	❑	❑	❑	6.	Your parent's behavior is getting more and more scary. You're afraid someone will get hurt.

3. Learning Self-Protection Skills: Skills and Information to Take Care of Myself

Making Good Choices and Knowing How to Say No

One of the first decisions to clear up is what are you going to do with alcohol and other drugs? Most teenagers are pressured by classmates and peers to drink alcohol or take other drugs. Your response to this peer pressure could have a lot to do with how your life turns out. If you are a child of an alcoholic, you are at four times greater risk of becoming an alcoholic later in life. Teenage drinking only increases the chance of becoming "hooked" on alcohol and experiencing a life of pain due to alcoholism. So, our wholehearted advice is: **Be smart. Don't start!**

In spite of all the TV commercials that send the message that good times and alcohol go together, there is life without alcohol. Many people choose not to drink (more than you would imagine) and are very happy. You can, too.

The *Just Say No Club* with which you are likely familiar has four promises that would be a good motto by which to live regardless of your age. Perhaps you are too old to be in the *Just Say No Club*, but the four guiding ideas of the club below are timeless.

1. I promise to be the best *me* I can be.
2. I promise to resist bad peer pressure.
3. I promise if I ever have a problem that I cannot handle myself, I'll talk it over with a trusted adult.
4. I promise if I ever have a scared or uncomfortable feeling inside about doing something, I'll just say no.

Why not memorize these four promises and hide them in your heart? You'll find that they can work for you to make positive choices and to feel good about yourself.

Knowing when to say no is crucial. It's not as hard as you think to know when to say no. Ask yourself these two questions when making a decision.

Mental Checklist

1. Is it (what I'm tempted to do) against the law or rules?

2. Will it hurt me or another person?

If the answer is yes to either of these questions, then you probably should *not* do it. Having a good sense of self-control is necessary to keep yourself safe, happy and out of trouble. A bad decision today can cost you the rest of your life. Stop and think of yourself!

Knowing *how* to say no is another issue when confronted with peer pressure. Try to put into practice the following ideas. You can get very good at taking care of yourself and not getting talked into things that are not in your best interest.

Assertive Responses

1. Look the person right in the eyes.

2. Speak up.

3. Say no right away and walk away.

4. Don't explain or apologize.

5. Mean what you say and say what you mean.

You may want to memorize a statement like the following and use it as needed.

"When you keep pressuring me to do something that I don't want to do, it makes me think you don't care about me."

Practical Tips for Taking Care of Yourself

When a person drinks too much, the home can become unstable and unpredictable. Using your head can make all the difference between being safe or hurt. When a person is acting in a way that scares you, try the following.

Home Safety Tips

1. Go to a place where you are out of the way such as your bedroom.

2. If necessary, go to a neighbor's home. (Work out a safe place to go ahead of time, such as a friend's or relative's home.)

3. Know safety routes out of the home if you need to get away. These safety routes are good to know in case of fire or violent behavior.

4. Have phone numbers of friends and relatives you can call for help. *Call 911* if you feel you or your family is in a dangerous situation. The police or sheriff can quickly assist your family.

5. Even when you are angry and feel you are being treated unfairly, *do not* argue or talk back. You cannot reason with someone who has had too much to drink.

6. Remember your support team. Stay near other family members for comfort and safety. There is safety in numbers.

One of the most dangerous situations to find yourself in is in a car after someone has been drinking. This puts you in a life threatening situation because alcohol greatly slows down the driver's reaction time and ability to think clearly. Therefore, try the following if you find yourself in a car with a person who has been drinking.

Car Safety Tips

1. If at all possible, do not get into the car. Tell the driver that you feel scared about riding in the car because of your concern about drinking and driving.

2. Always take coins to use at a pay phone to arrange for another ride if needed.

3. If you must get into the car, sit in the back seat and put on your seat belt.

4. Remain quiet. Do not argue or back talk with the driver.

Child Abuse Prevention and Protection

Child abuse is another concern. When people drink too much, they often are not thinking clearly. An alcoholic may yell a lot and hurt the feelings of others. An alcoholic may also hit or touch you in ways that hurt or make you feel uncomfortable. In general there are four types of child abuse.

Verbal Abuse

Verbal abuse involves saying mean or unkind things to another. Often when alcoholics are angry, they may yell, scream and even use curse words. Alcoholics may regret or feel sorry for their actions later. While drinking, they may be out of control and say things like:

"You'll never amount to anything."

"You're stupid."

"I wish you were never born."

Keep in mind these probably aren't the true feelings of the person who is drinking. Alcohol has a powerful grip on the person. Try this when unkind words are directed at you.

1. Give yourself clear messages such as "I'm an OK person," or "I'll get through this situation."

2. Don't believe for a minute the putdowns and negative comments. Block them out of your mind.

3. Don't talk back or yell at the alcoholic.

4. Move away to a safer place.

5. Try to forgive the alcoholic. Think of him or her as a very sick person who needs help from a doctor or other health professional.

Physical Abuse

Verbal abuse can quickly turn into physical abuse. Physical abuse involves hitting another. Physical abuse is very dangerous causing marks, bumps, bruises, or even broken bones. A person's life may be at risk when behavior turns violent. Therefore, you need to follow the safety rules if you find yourself in this situation. They are as follows:

1. Get away immediately.

2. Tell someone as soon as possible about what has happened. If you feel your health or others are at risk, *call 911.* Tell people in your support team such as your school counselor, a teacher, a friend's mother, and so forth.

3. Yell for help if necessary.

Some children feel afraid to tell. One thing for sure, the problem will just continue to occur unless you tell a trusted adult. Social workers can assist your family in getting the help you need. Remember the alcoholic needs help, so don't feel like you are getting the person in trouble. The alcoholic must face the consequences of his or her behavior, and *you deserve to be protected.*

Sexual Abuse

Sexual abuse can be a problem in some homes. When a person, usually someone who is much older, attempts to touch your private parts for no good reason, this is called sexual abuse. We're not talking about a doctor giving a physical examination or another appropriate reason. If someone ever tries to undress you or touch you in ways that cause you to feel hurt or uncomfortable, it is necessary for you to use the safety rules to protect yourself. You have the right to:

1. Say: "No, don't do that," or "Leave me alone."

2. Get away.

3. Tell someone in your support team.

4. Yell for help if you need to do so.

If you are ever or have been sexually abused in the past, remember it is not your fault. To make sure it doesn't continue, get help. By telling a trusted adult, a social worker will assist you and your family to stop the sexual abuse and to help make things better. Remember, anyone who would touch you in wrong ways needs help. You also deserve to be treated with respect.

Neglect

      The final type of abuse is neglect. When children do not receive proper care, they are being neglected. There are three basic needs—food, shelter, and clothing. Other needs include medical attention and medicine when a person is sick or hurt. Sometimes the alcoholic may spend much of the money for family needs on alcohol. As a result, the whole family may suffer. Again, if your basic needs are not being met, it is appropriate to let someone you trust know of your needs. Many people are glad to assist and help make sure your needs are met.

      In general, take good care of yourself by making good choices. Don't be afraid to talk, trust, and express your feelings to people in your support team. As difficult as your situation may be, it will pass. You can and will make it through this time. Your faith, courage, and support team will carry you on to a better life of your own.

4. Feeling Better About Myself

A. Clear Messages

I'm thinking of a person who is very important and special. This person is someone you see every day. This person is also one of the most important friends you could ever have. Can you name this person?

The answer is *YOU!* Sometimes we forget to be thankful for the good things in our lives when we are confused with family problems. One thing to keep in mind is that very few families are perfect. Feeling sad all the time is unproductive and will hurt your self-esteem.

The best way to feel better about yourself is to change your way of thinking. Your thinking gets you into trouble. It can also get you out of trouble. You have basically two ways of thinking about yourself and the things that happen to you. We call them muddy messages and clear messages.

Muddy messages are thoughts that cause you to feel bad about yourself. You feel upset inside and things bother you.

Clear messages are just the opposite. Your thoughts make you feel good about yourself. You feel at peace inside and things don't bother you.

Here are some examples of clear versus muddy thinking.

Event	Muddy Message	Clear Message
Someone calls you a name.	"Everyone thinks I'm a jerk."	"People who call names are just trying to get others upset. I'm not going to pay attention to him."
You failed a test.	"What's the point in trying? I'll never pass this class. I'm dumb in math."	"I wish I would have done better. However, I'm still an O.K. person. I'll get some help and do better next time."

This is called *self-talk*. What you say to yourself makes all the difference. To feel good about yourself, it is important to think good thoughts. Good thoughts equal good feelings. Remember we all have things we're not really good at doing. It is okay not to be good at some things. What's important is to do your best and learn to like yourself.

One of the most important self-talk words to remember is *IALAC*. It stands for I Am Lovable and Capable. *Lovable* means people can love you just because of who you are. You are special not because of what you do but who you are. *Capable* means you can. You can do many things well. Take a minute to list at least two things you do well at school and outside of school.

In School	**Out of School**
1. _____	1. _____
2. _____	2. _____

On an index card, write the word IALAC. Let this be your secret code word. Take it with you to remind you that you are special and O.K.

IALAC is a wonderful clear message. There are many more that you can say to yourself. Try the following experiment this week. Every time something happens to you good or bad, give yourself a clear message. Catch your muddy messages and change them to clear messages. Remember, you control what you think. No junk thoughts! Practice using clear messages such as:

"I'm O.K."

"I can handle it."

"I'll just do my best."

"No one is perfect."

"It's going to work out."

List some more clear messages you might give yourself.

1. _____

2. _____

3. _____

4. _____

B. RAS Your Feelings

When it comes to feelings, you have all kinds. It is important to know how to handle feelings. The word RAS is another secret code word worth remembering. It can remind you of three important things to do with your feelings.

R stands for **Recognize Your Feelings.**

Recognize means to know or to think about your feelings. You have two types of feelings. Here are some examples under each type.

Pleasant Feelings	Unpleasant Feelings
(Feelings we like to have)	(Feelings we don't like to have)
A. happy	G. sad
B. excited	H. mad
C. surprised	I. frustrated
D. loved	J. disappointed
E. confident	K. scared
F. hopeful	L. guilty
	M. embarrassed
	N. worried

Recognizing or knowing what feelings you have is very important. Throughout each day, stop for a minute and listen to your feelings. Ask, how am I feeling right now? Your body and mind will tell you.

For one entire week, using the chart on the next page, take a minute in the morning, after school, and before bed to identify your strongest feeling. Pick a feeling word from the list of pleasant and unpleasant feelings and put the letter in the appropriate box. At the end of the week add up how often each letter or feeling occurred.

A stands for **Accept Your Feelings.**

Accept means that your feelings are always O.K. Accept means to take your feelings as they are. There is nothing wrong with feeling the way you do. Feelings are a part of you, and they are O.K.

S stands for **Share Your Feelings**

Feelings are to be **shared** with others. Talking to people you trust about your feelings is a wonderful way to express your feelings. Feelings are not to be kept inside. You just feel better when you talk to others about your feelings. Who can you share your feelings with? Try to list at least three people whom you believe can be trusted with your deepest feelings.

Chart My Feelings

Time	Monday	Tuesday	Wednesday	Thursday	Friday	Saturday	Sunday
Morning							
Afternoon							
Evening							

- Write the letter for your strongest feeling three times a day for one week.
- Add up how often each feeling occurred
- Read section 5 of this book

5. Taking Control of My Life: Making Good Choices to Make My Life Better

A. Using Your Head and Heart

The first decision you need to make is that you *are* going to take care of yourself.

Perhaps your best two weapons are your head and heart. Your head, of course, involves using your brain power to make good decisions about how to act. Your heart is used to give you feelings about whether to do something or not. It is important to know how to listen to your feelings.

To use your *head*, always ask yourself these three questions before doing anything:

1. What am I getting ready to do?
2. What will happen if I do this?
3. What can I do instead?

Write these questions on a 3X5 inch index card or a small piece of paper. Carry it with you or tape it on your desk until you know them well. This card can be your "control card."

Using your heart means listening or "tuning in" to your feelings. Your feelings are important and shouldn't be ignored. Try this: Write down the following promise used in the *Just Say No Club* on another card or sheet of paper.

Just Say No Promise #4

"I promise, if I ever have a scared, uncomfortable feeling inside about doing something, I'll just say no."

When you have the uh-oh feeling inside, your heart is telling you there is something wrong. Listen to your heart and think about doing the right thing.

Take the time to use your head and your heart. They are like two good friends. The split second it takes to think clearly and to notice your feelings will make the difference in getting along in school or not. It's up to you. You can control your behavior.

B. Listing Problem Areas or Life's Struggles

In order to take control of your life, you need to decide which of your personal worries are within or out of your control. The first step in doing this is to actually list the things that get you down and make you sad. Think for a few minutes and write all of your worries below.

1. _____
   _____

2. _____
   _____

3. _____
   _____

4. _____
   _____

5. _____
   _____

6. _____
   _____

C. Reality Check

It is a good idea to divide your personal worries into two categories. (Those worries that you feel you have some control over and those worries which you probably can't change no matter how hard you try.)

List your personal worries again, but this time write the worries that you feel you *can* control on the front burners of the stove top on page 60. Next list your personal worries that you feel you *can not* control on the back burners of the stove top.

Look on page 59 for an example of how this might be done.

This drawing can be helpful to you when you try to stay focused in a positive way at home and school.

Here is an example:

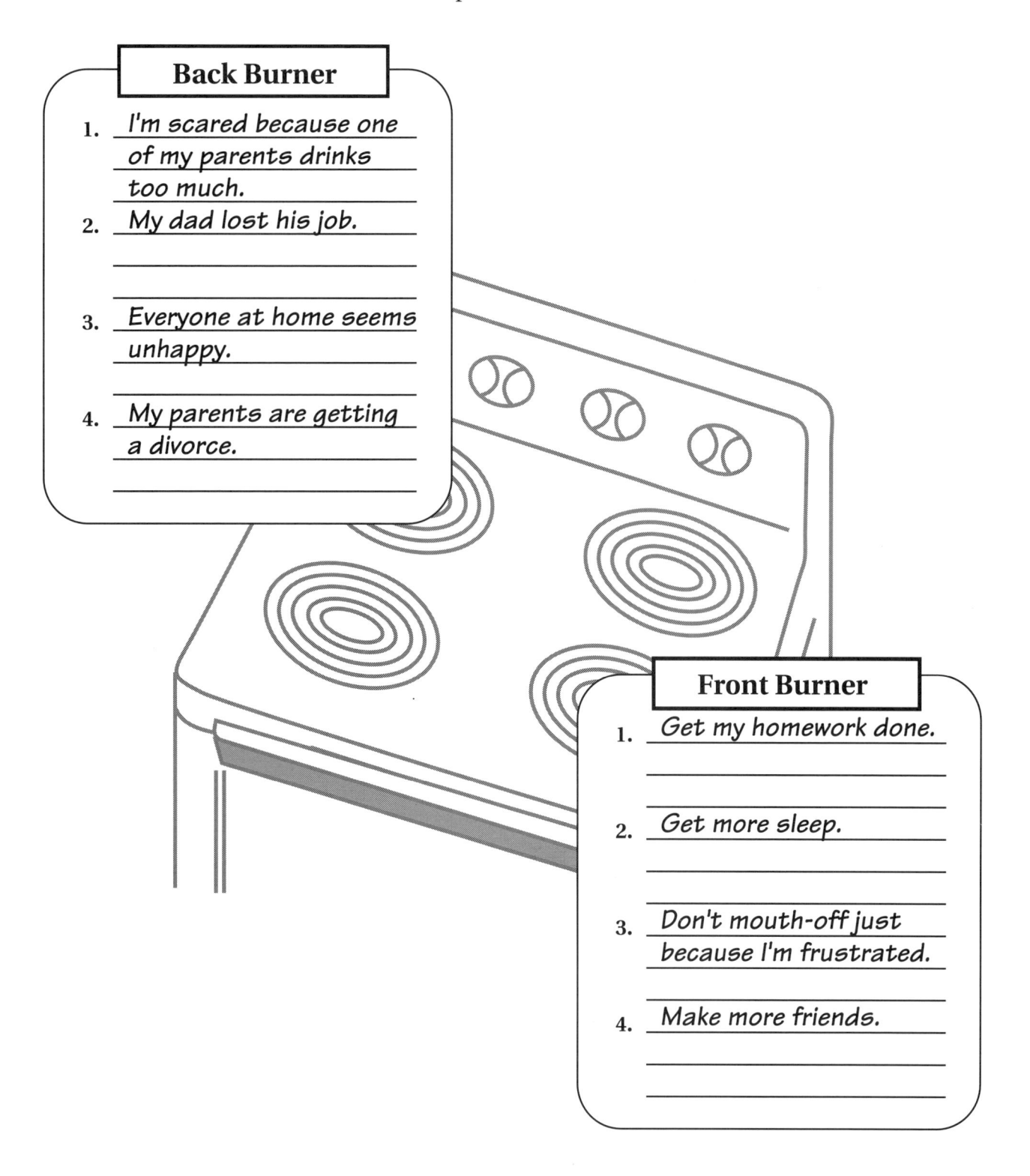

Back Burner

1. I'm scared because one of my parents drinks too much.
2. My dad lost his job.
3. Everyone at home seems unhappy.
4. My parents are getting a divorce.

Front Burner

1. Get my homework done.
2. Get more sleep.
3. Don't mouth-off just because I'm frustrated.
4. Make more friends.

Getting a Life of Your Own

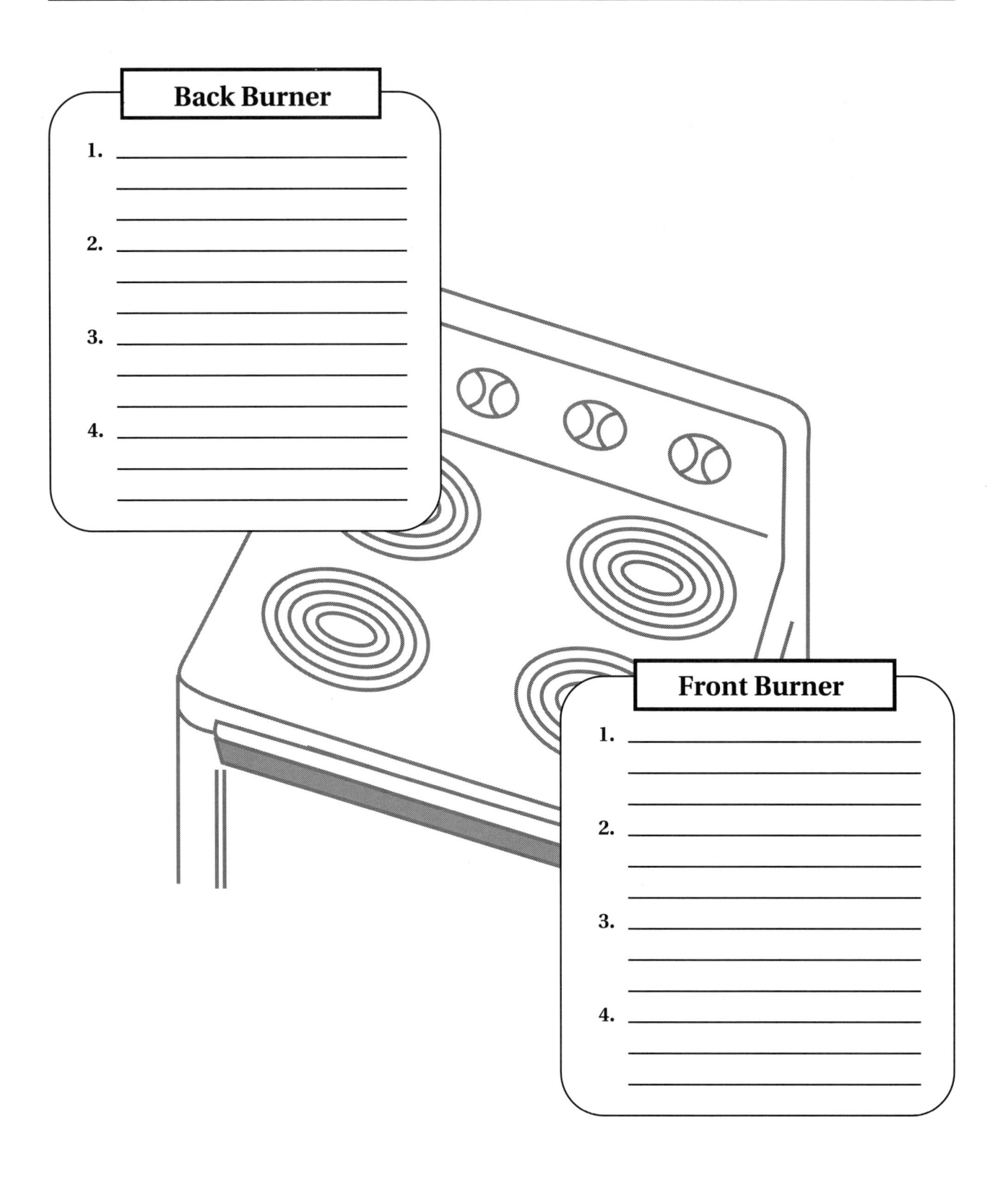

Back Burner

1. _____
2. _____
3. _____
4. _____

Front Burner

1. _____
2. _____
3. _____
4. _____

The worries that you listed on the back burners don't mean that you don't care or don't want things to change. It just means that these worries are situations that at this time in your life will probably be there for a long time; and if they are taken off of the stove as a result of time or other circumstances, it probably wasn't a result of your actions.

The worries that you listed on the front burners are concerns that you can probably change with effort. These are concerns on which you *should* focus your energy.

Ask yourself the following questions:
1. What is it that you really want to change?

2. What are you doing now about the situation?

3. Are you willing to talk to people on your support team to make a plan that will help you get what you want?

4. Will you list at least three (3) specific things you can start to do to get or accomplish what you really want?
    1. _____
    2. _____
    3. _____
    4. _____
    5. _____

These steps are good things to talk over with a trusted adult in your support team. While you have the ability to work out problems in your life, it is good to connect with an older person to review your plan.

Good Luck and Remember—*You can get a life of your own.*

References

Children of alcoholics: Facts and figures. (1992, May/June). *The Big Issue, 20*(3). Columbia, SC: South Carolina Department of Alcohol and Other Drug Abuse Services.

Frank, K.E., & Smith, S.J. (1993). *Children of alcoholics.* Rock Hill, SC: Winthrop University.

Frank, K.E., & Smith, S.J. (1994). *Getting a grip on ADD: A kids's guide to understanding and coping with attention disorders.* Minneapolis, MN: Educational Media Corporation.

Smith, S.J., & Walter, G. (1988). *Four steps to making friends.* Rock Hill, SC: Winthrop University.

Notes

Notes